A JOURNEY OF WORDS AND RHYMES

Ronald J. Hammond

The Cover:
L&M Creations
Osceola, MO 64776
pozzi82244@gmail.com

L & M Creations
Osceola, MO 64776
417-646-1393

A JOURNEY OF WORDS AND RHYMES

For more information, please write:
Ronald James Hammond
hammondronnie1@gmail.com

This book is a gathering of verses written by the author.

Manufactured in the United States of America.

-- Dedication --

This book is dedicated to teachers,
professors, friends, and family who
have
taught, encouraged, and stood
behind me
with my poetry writing.
To God be the glory for He has
given me this wonderful gift!

Ronnie James Hammond

Table of Contents

I.
Cowboys and Rodeos

"Racing Against the Clock"

The steer leaves the chute in a flash
suddenly it's a mad dash,
Your mount bounds out of the box
as quick as a fox,
You start swinging your rope
racing against time there's still hope,
You let go with a throw
and around both horns the rope rolls,
You quickly dally down
with a grin, not a frown,
Your heeler does his deal
and comes up with both heels,
Time quits racing
and now, each other, you're facing,
You have just beat time
and my, it feels fine!

Ronnie "The Poet" Hammond
1994

"The Barrel Racer"

They seemingly fly through the gate, a blurred vision
just horse and rider, on a timed mission,
Running across the disked dirt
the rider's entry number still pinned to her shirt,
They make the first turn
with little, or no concern,
Then, they make the second turn
while time continues to burn,
The horse and rider turn one last time
as if, on a dime,
Then, they head for the finish line, without time to pout
meanwhile, the fans continue to scream and shout
but she is the winner, there's no doubt!

Ronnie "The Poet" Hammond
3-5-1995

"The Right Mind"

With a leap and a bound
they explode from the chute, and start spinning around
Free-arm in the air
the rider hasn't time to worry or care,
Since the opening of the gate
he's had his mind set on eight,
Hoping the judges aren't blind
he remains right in his mind,
Until at last, the whistle finally blows
and his face begins to beam and glow,
While the fans applaud and cheer
he's faced the beast and his fears,
And now the score he hears.

Ronnie "The Poet" Hammond
2-27-1995

"Bull Poker"

After the release forms are filled-out
the contestants anxiously pace about,
Until, into the arena they are called
full of stupidity, or maybe nerve and Gaul,
Around the table they sit playing cards
but staying in a chair, with a bull on the prowl, is hard.
3o, some quickly get up and head for the gate
while others wait to meet their fate,
The lucky one walks away with the cash
while the unfortunate, make an emergency room dash,
This dangerous game would be loved by the "Joker"
and it is called, "Bull Poker!"

Ronnie "The Poet" Hammond
7-13-99

"The Cowboy Life-Saver"

He paints his face white
for decoration, not fright,
Then, he adds color to his eyes
and a big, red smile for a cheerful surprise,
Finally, he paints on a few tear drops that run down his cheek
these give him a look of sadness so bleak,
After his face is painted, he puts on his shirt and clothes
some shirts sparkle, and others glow,
His shorts are cut-off Wranglers way to big
so that when he dances, he can groove and dig,
Around his waist are colorful bandannas hanging tied
the bandannas are to wipe a tear from a cowboy's eye,
On his legs are tights with pads on the knees
in a bad situation, the pads he will need,
As well as the shoes on his feet, that are lined with cleats
when he enters the arena, he is a sight that is comical and neat,
For a cowboy he would lay down his life as a favor
fore' he is the cowboy life-saver!

Ronnie "The Poet" Hammond
9-11-97

Ronnie Hammond

"A Cowboy's Hero"

Around his waist hang his chaps
while on his head rests a beat-up Stetson hat,
A lariat hangs from the horn
while his face wears an expression of scorn,
His spurs jingle as his horse trots along
in the rodeo arena they both belong,
Their job is to rescue bronc and bareback riders
although the riders are a tough race of fighters
He is a fellow so tall and lanky
and tied around his neck waves a red hanky,
So when the riders make the whistle, and are seeking safety
it makes no difference, whether they're slim or hefty,
The pickup man will be there in a bound
to safely set them on the ground,
Even though the pickup man doesn't receive a score of 100 or zero
to the cowboy, he is still a hero!

Ronnie "The Poet" Hammc
9-15-97

"The Calf-Scramble"

Into the arena, children are called
over dirt clods, they sometimes fall.
In all shapes and sizes they are
wanting to make some money, and be a star
The clowns put them all in a line
where they exercise until they're told it's time,
Then, the calves are turned loose
and the kids vamoose,
Ribbons tied on the calves tails they chase
keeping a frantic pace,
Until, the ribbons are all retrieved
and the weary calves relieved,
To the judges, the winners dash
and turn in their ribbon, for a $1.00 in cash,
For everyone involved, it was a gamble
but that's all part of the calf-scramble!

Ronnie "The Poet" Hammoı
7-12-99

"The Posting of Western Colors"

One flag represents the contractor of stock
the other, the rodeo associations that is held in a
stirrup prop.
The pick-up men circle the arena, on different sides at a walk
as the announcer continues to talk,
Then, halfway round, they are asked to, "Post the colors
western style"
and, the flags ripple and wave, all the while,
The horses snort and run
in the heat of the afternoon sun,
Until, in the center, they're brought to a stop
while riders are introduced, the horses prance and hop,
Then, after all is said and done
they leave the arena at a run,
Behind them, clods of dirt are hurled
as dust devils disappear in a whirl!

Ronnie "The Poet" Hammond
7-13-99

"The Grand Entry"

Into the arena they ride
with their heads held high,
The sun is almost down
and the announcer's voice is the only sound
As he talks of rodeo traditions, of long ago
a warm summer breeze gently blows
Numbers pinned on shirt backs sway
as the riders circle the arena, riding away,
From boots and hats
to jeans and chaps,
There's a variety of colors, shapes and styles
that form a rainbow, as out of the gate, they file,
While the announcer watches from horseback, like a sentry
so ends another "Grand Entry"

Ronnie "The Poet" Hammond
7-13-99

"My Old Gray Boots"

They sit on the porch all ragged and worn
scratches on the toes with one side torn,
Their heels are uneven, loose, and thin
from being worn to school, on rides, and in cattle pens,
The sides no longer stiff and straight
are falling over like their mate,
A gray, snake skin appearance had once shown,
but to a life of hard work they were prone,
Worn through rain, mud, and snow
the price paid years ago was low,
I might buy a new pair, if I had the loot
but it would be hard to say, "bye,"
." to my old gray boots!

Ronnie "The Poet" Hammond
10-13-99

"Posse"

Deputized by the Sheriff, to help uphold the law,
Horses saddled, bridled, and freshly shod,
Shotguns, rifles, and pistols checked, and filled with shells,
Bandanna's, hats, and slickers are gotten, in case the weather isn't swell,
Goodbye's are quickly said to loved ones,
Then, it's into saddles, and in pursuit of crooks on the run,
Come day or night, they stop long enough to eat, and rest,
So as to be prepared for a confrontation, and pass the test,
If push comes to shove, leather will be slapped,
And in blankets, dead bodies will be wrapped,
However, if they surrender, cuffs and ankle shackles will be applied,
Then, back to town, where court will be held, to find the truth, or lies,
Either way, they are determined, and even bossy,
'fore, they are a deputized posse!

Ronnie "The Poet" Hammond
02-18-2017

"The Native People"

Once they stood majestic as an eagle
and their weapons were lethal,
They lived beside rivers and streams
while with their shaman, they talked of visitors and dreams
Back then, they were free as the wind
with spirits you could not bend
Painting their faces while wearing buckskin with fringe
when seen, their enemies would cringe,
Their hair, in long, black braids
only with age, would fade,
Wearing moccasins on golden, tan feet
at festivals, around bonfires, they would dance to drum beats
In battle, scalps they would take
and portable homes, they would make,
Through the woods, they'd ride
sometimes on the run, and looking for a place to hide,
All they ever wanted, was to live in peace!

Ronnie "The Poet" Hammond
1994

"The Smitty"

As the sun begins to rise

a weary smitty wipes the sweat from his eyes,

An old mare

with coal black hair,

Stands tied to a tree

while birds begin to sing,

Aching with pain

and nothing to gain,

The smitty continues to do his job

with no time to sob,

With dew on his boots

an owl continues to hoot,

Shaping the shoe

he hears doves coo,

Ready to put in nails

he knows he cannot fail,

He finishes the mare

with kind, gentle care,

His broad shoulders and back soaked with sweat

there's no need to fret,

For his work is now complete.

Ronnie "The Poet" Hammond
5-11-1993

"The Cattle Driver's"

For weeks they've plodded along
with throats so dry, they can't carry a song,
Dusty, dry, and long is the trail
driving the steers to market,
they mustn't fail,
Facing all kinds of dangers, they continue their quest
'fore once reunited with their families they will be blessed,
Those without families will forever be on a drive
'til the day comes that they die,
So onward they travel
until time seems to unravel,
Around the campfire they exchange glances
remembering other drives and ranches,
With aching bodies they sleep on the cold, hard ground at night
and rise with the first rays of light,
These were rough and rugged men no doubt
'cause they went through hell for pay that was small in amount!

Ronnie "The Poet" Hammond
12-21_96

"Stampede"

We were on the trail with a 1,000 herd of longhorns
when thunder began to clap, and the sky was torn
The wind began to fiercely blow
as lightning set the sky aglow,
Then the rain began to fall
while the steers grew nervous and bawled,
A tree hit by lightning exploded with a horrendous boom
for the drovers this meant certain doom,
The steers stampeded and ran across the prairie
while the drovers horses continued to catch up with the
loads they carried,
Some drovers got in front of the herd and were tromped
as across the dry, hard ground the steers stomped
Hours later, the herd began to tire
while drovers pistols were fired,
The herd then settled down and turned back
and once again the drovers hit the sack!

Ronnie "The Poet" Hammond
3-19-1996

"The Drive"

The cattle are driven along the sun-scorched trail,
buzzards circle overhead, knowing that, "Death" will not fail,
Everything slowly lumbers along,
in hopes, of finding a river, creek, or pond,
With little grass to eat, and, no shade in sight,
some won't make it, others might,
The cow-pokes are tired, sore, and alone,
knowing they are a hundred miles from home,
They would have rather stayed home, and been boss during the day,
but, with fall coming on, they all need their pay,
So, after the drive is over, and the cattle are sold,
each man will try to make it home, before the weather turns cold,
But, the nearest town will be visited first,
to find a gift for their Mrs, and to quench their thirst,
Then, they will saddle a fresh horse, and for home, they'll ride,
'fore next spring will bring a new herd to drive!

Ronnie "The Poet" Hammond
8-19-2000

"The Trail"

The trail is dusty and hot
with no shade or cool spots,
The dust blows thick and dry
and the birds no longer fly,
The longhorns move without haste
with very little green grass to taste,
The days grow busy, roping and branding
until no steer is left standing,
The nights are spent with tales told
of earlier herds bought and sold,
We turn in for sleep, our stomach full of biscuits and beans
and our slumber is filled with thoughts and dreams,
Until the early morning comes
as if to the beat of a drum,
We turn to the trail again.

Ronnie "The Poet" Hammond
1994

"Pursuit of the Posse?"

An outlaw on the lam,
Riding through lands untamed.
Behind him a posse is in pursuit,
Their horses running, and snorting, like wild beasts,
Hell bent for leather,
Regardless of the weather,
To the ends of the Earth, they'll ride if need be,
With no regard to the scenery they might see,
While the wind blows in their faces,
Riding through canyons, and open spaces,
When they catch this outlaw man,
He'll go before the judge on the stand,
If guilty, he'll sit in a cell, wasting and rotting away,
Or, from the gallows, he'll hang till his feet no longer sway,
Either way, the bandit will no longer steal or be bossy,
Thanks to the Sheriff, and the pursuit of the posse!

Ronnie "The Poet" Hammond
11-25-2016

II. History and Fantasy

"A Matador's Day"

Into the arena they enter as a parade,
waiting for the cheers of the fans to fade,
Matadors dressed in traditional, "suits of lights,"
stroll around, much to the fans delight,
Soon the riders vamoose,
and the bull is turned loose,
Alone with a cloth that is red,
the matador prays that he won't end up dead,
Then, like a ballerina, he spins around,
his feet, seemingly off the ground,
While with the cloth of red,
he blinds the bull, by throwing it over his head,
After about 20 minutes elapse,
the bull will die and collapse,
A victim of the matador's sword,
just so the fans wouldn't be bored
So, to the cheers of, "Ole,
the matador ends his day!

Ronnie "The Poet" Hammond

10-5-99

"A Cavalry Officer"

He stands straight and proud,
Attentive in silence, not being loud,
Clean shaven and well groomed,
Showing no sign of fear, dismay, or gloom,
A long sleeve white shirt is covered by a dark blue jacket,
Insignia bars on each shoulder tells his rank, like in a bracket,
Two rows of brass buttons come down each side,
Yellowish trim around the cuffs, he will not hide,
Around the waist is a black, leather belt, with a buckle,
Long white gloves cover his hands, and knuckles,
A saber hangs from his left side, and a pistol on the right,
Never taking chances, always prepared for a fight,
Lighter blue trousers with a long, yellow stripe on the outside of each leg,
If death comes, he'll die in honor, and not beg,
His boots are tall, shiny, and black,
Adorned with a spur on each heel, nothing left to lack,
Believing in destiny, not fate,
He is a Calvary officer of the United States!

Ronnie "The Poet" Hammond
1-14-17

"PIRATES"

On the high seas, they fearlessly sailed,

Not afraid to face any challenge or peril,

Some were short, others were tall,

Hard-headed, and determined to not fall,

Most had mustaches, and big beards,

Mean, and cruel, they were to be feared,

To receive a black spot was a death like warning,

More than likely, you'd be dead by the morning,

Aboard a ship, you'd be forced to walk the plank,

Regardless of what you say or think,

With big hats, and clothes, they were a rough batch,

Some with wooden peg legs, others with an eye patch,

Plundering and looting was their claim to fame,

Looking for gold, gems, and other things to claim,

A black flag, with a skull and crossbones, flew high above their ship,

While across the seas they sailed on another adventurous trip!

Ronnie "The Poet" Hammond
10-07-16

"THE GAMBLER"

At a dimly lit table he sits,
Against the other players, he has only his wits,
Clean shaven, and dressed to the hilt,
Being lucky and smooth is how his reputation is built,
Shiny boots, and dark colored slacks,
A long sleeve, white shirt, with a vest of gray and black,
Around his neck is a black tie,
Are tales he tells, the truth, or a lie?
slid back atop his head is a cowboy hat of gray,
A boyish smile he has during the day,
Quickly, he shuffles, cuts, and deals the cards,
While the piano players, and men drink at the bar,
Cards are secretly viewed, and bets are made,
To be superior, and for the money he plays,
Does he hold a full house, a royal flush, or 4 aces?
The suspense can be seen in the other player's faces,
Two drop out, and the last decides to call
Unfortunately for him, the gambler set him up for a fall,
With keen dancing eyes, and a sly, little smirk,
He reaches out over the table, and rakes in the perks,
From town to town he is a rambler,
For he is a card playing gambler!

Ronnie "The Poet" Hammond
10-15-16

"THE DUEL"

Tempers flare, and internal flames refuse to fade,
A slap in the face with a glove, and a challenge is made,
The day comes, and the two participants arrive,
Each knowing that only one may possibly survive,
Pick your weapon of choice, each is told,
* Pistols are chosen, a lethal choice, so bold,
Back to back they bravely stand,
Then, counting 30 paces, they walk across the land,
At the command, on the last step, they turn,
Firing at each other, only one feels the bullets burn,
Whether he lives or dies depends on the others aim,
If poor, he'll tell the tale of how close to death he came,
A good shot to the heart and chest,
Will take his life, and lay him to rest,
To lose their tempers and become so sore, they are both fools,
'Cause no good comes to either one, when they duel!

Ronnie "The Poet" Hammond
10-18-16

"Vikings"

Tall and strong, with long hair and thick beards,
to face any man or beast, they had no fear.
Fierce warriors, united together, they'd take a stand.
against enemies on their home soil, or on distant lands.
Across the seas in ships they'd sail,
with no thoughts of turning back, or to fail.
Long, broad swords and battle axes by their sides,
parts of their bodies covered with animal furs, and hides.
Upon their heads sat metal helmets, some with horns,
charms, or pendants around their necks were adorned
Some had wooden shields on an arm,
to block a foes blows, and protect them from harm.
Around a campfire in their native tongue they'd speak
while fresh killed animals they'd roast and eat.
Entering battles with savage warrior cries,
as foes and friends alike, bled and died.
By exploring new places they did their part,
and in the history books, left their mark.
Sooner or later they were bound to disappear, or take a fall,
these proud warriors, or "Vikings,"as they were called!

Ronnie "The Poet" Hammond
10-25-16

"Gladiators"

While the sun hangs high in the sky,
They enter the arena to the crowd's applause, and cries,
Their sandals walk across the blood stained sand,
With tridents, swords, axes, and nets in hand,
Helmets on heads, and little body armor to wear,
Each swing of an arm brings danger, they must take care,
As they stand in place, the Emperor rises to his feet,
With his hands he quiets the crowd so he can speak,
The afternoon's games are a fight to the death,
Until only 1 remains standing, and able to take a breath,
After the Emperor says, "Begin," the battle ensues,
4 gladiators fight for survival while battled, bloodied, and bruised,
One falls with a sword through his chest,
Tired and sore, the first cannot afford to rest,
A second is speared with a trident while snared in a net,
Blood drips off the opponents arms, mixed with sweat,
Now, only 2 gladiators remain,
Pulling out all stops, they will not refrain,

"Gladiators"

Continued

Sword clings and clangs with the head of the axe,

The contest ends with a chop, and a hack,

As the crowd applauds, and roars in bloody delight,

Wanting more bloodshed, and another fight,

The lone survivor limps back to the holding room,

Weak, injured, and with little refreshment or food,

If he awakes from sleep this night,

Training will resume until the next fights,

Walking out, or being carried away,

The latter will happen someday,

Careful to obey the rules, and not be branded a traitor,

He is proud to be part of the brotherhood, called Gladiator!

Ronnie "The Poet" Hammond
10-27-16

"Mountain Man"

Towards the end of summer he heads to the mountains and hills,

Each new sunrise finds him closer to the mountain's chill,

Riding his horse and leading a pack mule,

With provisions, traps, and weapons, he's no fool,

Clothes made of buckskin with a coonskin cap,

He can't wait to get to the rivers and set his muskrat and beaver traps,

Moccasin style boots are on his feet, with a Bowie knife and pistol on his side,

A mustache and full beard are on his face, and his hearts full of pride,

Battling the elements, and racing against time,

Neither Indians or obstacles will keep him from reaching the pines,

Once there, he'll build a makeshift shelter to keep him safe and warm at night,

Then, begins the long days of running trap lines at daylight,

Cleaning, scraping, stretching, and tanning hides,

Thinking of items he can hopefully trade for, or buy,

All season he works and lives all alone,

He may never see a person, or even scattered bones,

Surviving, with what he can off of the land,

Careful when setting steel traps, to not catch his fingers or hands

Through the wind, rain, snow, and numbing cold,

He continues his work, ever so bold,

"Mountain Man"

Continued

Season closes, and to civilization he makes the trek,

Hoping his hides and furs will bring top money, and get him a fat check,

A few more good seasons, and he hopes to be set,

With enough money to settle down and enjoy what years he has left,

To be tame, he doesn't know if he can,

For in his heart, he'll always be a, "Mountain Man!"

Ronnie "The Poet" Hammond
10-30-16

"Robin Hood"

Joining the Crusades was Richard the Lion Heart,

He believed in the cause and was doing his part,

But in his absence, his brother seized control and was greedy,

Caring not about the loyal subjects, and people's needs,

Having the Sheriff of Nottingham do his dirty deeds,

Until one man decided to take a stand, and be free,

Clothed in green, and an archer supreme,

In any shooting contest, of the crop, he was the cream,

Gathering together a merry band of men,

They protected the people from taxes, and sin,

From Nottingham Castle to Sherwood Forest they rode,

Taking from the rich, to give to the poor, how bold,

Robin of Locksley did what was right whenever he could,

How cunning and crafty a leader he was as, "

"Robin Hood!"

Ronnie "The Poet" Hammond

1-01-20

"Genie of the Lamp"

Buried in a desert for thousands of years,
Never to be found thought the owner, he had no fear,
Years later discovered by accident, and dug up,
A bronze colored lamp, not a cup,
On the side was an engraved inscription,
That read, "Rub three times," but, no other description,
Following the directions, with a rub of the hand three times,
Out of the tiny spout came a mist type smoke so fine,
As it rose into the air a figure appeared,
From the waist up, a muscular genie with no fear,
Bald with a black pony tail, and blue eyes,
- Golden bracelets, on his wrists, brighter than the skies,
A voice like thunder when he spoke,
With your three wishes you can be rich or famous, no longer broke,
For now I am your slave, and your wish is my command,
But once your third wish is granted, I have only one demand,
Release me from the curse of the lamp,
Or I'Il remain trapped either hot, or cold, dry or damp,
An agreement reached, and a promise made,
Only time will tell if it's kept, or if his masters memory fades!

Ronnie "The Poet" Hammond
11-21-16

"The Reaper"

A pawn used by its master Death,
It takes the souls of people when they breathe their last breath,
Wearing a long, black hooded cloak, or robe,
What lies underneath, nobody knows,
A scythe will be used on you if you try to get away,
It moves unlike any human body can bend or sway,
Gliding across land, or floating through the air,
You better heed my warning, and take care,
Never needing food, water, or rest,
For this grisly job, it is the best,
Once captured, your soul is sent up high, or down below,
We know not if it's a woman, or a fellow,
No bargains can be made, or dues paid,
It's here to do a job, and will not go away, or fade,
Simply vanishing once its task is complete,
Truly one thing in life that you never want to meet,
Guaranteed to make you think, "Oh, Jeepers Creepers"
Trust me when I say, you better fear The Reaper!

Ronnie "The Poet' Hammond
February 7, 2017

"A Supreme Wizard"

In a tower of a stone castle he stays,
Working and experimenting, he has everyone keep away,
Jars and bottles hold roots, herbs, potions, and such things,
On a finger on his left hand is a glowing ring,
A long, flowing robe with planets and stars on it he wears,
His hat is tall and slim, how it looks, he doesn't care,
White-haired with a long, soft beard,
When his eyes flare up, he is too feared,
In the sash around his robe is where he keeps his wand,
Between them is a magical, mystical bond,
A book of spells lays on the counter top,
Flipping pages till he finds the right one, then he stops,
Mixing up all sorts of things, while reciting the spell out loud,
While clouds darken, and winds blow and howl,
Then, with a puff of smoke, the spell is complete,
To break its power, would be quite a feat,
Taking orders from any man, he will have no part,
Try and force him, and he'll stop your beating heart,
Come heat, wind, rain, or a blizzard,
Nothing stops him, or scares him, because he is a Supreme Wizard!

Ronnie "The Poet" Hammond
February 19, 2017

"Dragon Rider"

Red, scaly skin, with dark, green eyes,
Large, powerful wings that enable it to fly,
A long tail that is split at the end,
Sharp, black claws, keep dangers away, but not friends,
Spike looking horns rise out of its head,
It spits fire from its mouth, burning up everything where it lands,
A leather, saddle type contraption sits upon its back,
Leaping upon the beast, settling in the seat, and placing boots in stirrups,
With a sigh and leap, they take to the skies, like birds that chirp,
High in the sky amongst the clouds they fly,
Circling, gliding, and doing power dives,
Basking in the warmth of the sun,
Normally on a mission, seldom do they partake in fun,
Armed with a sword, hatchet, and bow,
It's death from above, or close to the ground so low,
Listen to my warning, and take heed,
If you cross their paths, let them do as they please,
Or you may find yourself battling a barbaric fighter,
And his dragon, because he is a Dragon Rider!

Ronnie 'The Poet' Hammond
February 19, 2017

"The Crystal Ball"

It sits in the center of a table,
To predict and see one's future, it is able,
A golden base holds it up off the table, and in place,
Be careful as you peer into it cause you may see a face,
The inside is filled with a smoke like substance,
That changes colors, and may leave you in a trance,
As you watch closely, the smoke swirls, and floats around,
Intently watching, you will hear no sound,
While the fortune teller works her magic and charm,
To be in a hurry, there is no need for alarm,
Will you live a long and healthy life?
Or be married to a beautiful wife?
Have riches and treasures beyond compare?
And maybe live in a mansion so fair?
As you think about your questions, be wise when you choose,
So as to not make a mistake, and possibly lose,
Hopefully your future will be positive and good, with no falls,
As you sit with the fortune teller around the crystal ball!

Ronnie 'The Poet' Hammond
November 22, 2016

"A Country Super Star"

He learned to play the guitar and sing,

Practicing at school, Church, and other places and things,

Soon it was nightclubs, taverns, and bars,

Wondering if he was good enough to go far,

A few years went by as he traveled around to different gigs,

Now, he was making a name, and starting to get big,

Finally, a call he received by phone,

And for a meeting in Nashville, he was flown,

A deal was made, and a contract signed,

Now, everything was coming together just fine,

After weeks of hard work, his first record was complete,

It went to the top of the country charts, what a feat!

A top star, it's now concerts and shows,

Seeing people from all over the world come and go,

Then to perform at the Grand Ole Opry, he got the invite,

And his heart filled with pride and delight

As he walks across the stage, and sits down on a stool,

Remembering someone that once turned him down and treated him like a fool,

"You're not country enough, and you'll never go far,

Smiling, he plays and sings, because he is a country super star!

Ronnie "The Poet' Hammond
November 18, 2016

"Secret Agent Man?"

Years of training and studying, he has been through,
From hand-to-hand combat, U.S. History, and even animals of the zoo,
Tactics and techniques, he has learned and used,
Avoiding drugs, tobacco, cigarettes, and booze,
Keeping his mind and body in tip-top shape,
Controlling his temper, not giving into hate,
A fast, sleek car is his ride,
Keeping it polished and waxed, he takes great pride,
Top of the line business suits he wears,
To remain clean shaven, he takes great care,
Cool gadgets come with the car, and the job,
A pistol, a laser pen, and gas that makes you cry and sob,
Microchips in the heel of his shoes,
And vehicle gadgets, some of which he hasn't a clue,
Fluent in more than one language as well,
He is highly educated, but his head doesn't swell,
On assignment he's traveled all over the world,
Withstanding car chases, knives, bullets, and grenades hurled,
For his country, and the flag, he'll do what he must,
Never giving up secrets, or your trust,
Always ready to do what's right, and take a stand,
He is a top secret agent man!

Ronnie "The Poet' Hammond
November 23, 2016

"SideKicks"

On the big screen with the leading man they rode,
They to, never lied, cheated, or stole,
Often times they provided humor, but sometimes saved the day,
Providing assistance whatever needed, even by feeding hay,
Sidekicks like, "Little Beaver," "Smiley Burnette," and, "Gabby Hayes,
Rode with, "Red Ryder," "Gene Autry," and " Roy Rogers," for days,
Several more I could talk about and name,
However the compliments would be more of the same,
They may not have been the leading man, with the biggest part,
But, they won over audiences, and still live in our hearts,
In our memories they will forever ride,
With the lead man, side by side,
Over, and over they paid their dues, and took their licks,
For they were cowboys, actors, and western sidekicks!

Ronnie "The Poet" Hammond
08-01-16

III.
Holidays

"Happy Easter"

Children running all around,

Looking for colored eggs on the ground,

Basket's full of candy with toys,

For all the Girl's and Boy's,

People attending Church, dressed in their best,

Hearing about His arising from his death,

Families gathering together to share a meal,

Few businesses open, and no making of deals,

A time to be together, and enjoy the day,

"Happy Easter," is all that's left to say!

Ronnie "The Poet" Hammond
03-26-16

"Snow Day Fun"

Through the front gate we go,
Our wooden sled tied to a rope, in tow,
Surveying the hillside and pond, we choose a route,
Taking turns, no one cries, or pouts,
Running and diving onto the sled, ice and snow sloshing as I go,
The colds not a factor, because we're bundled up from head to toe,
Twisting and turning, while slipping and sliding all the way,
Whooping, and yelling with delight, and nothing more to say,
Finally, the pond is reached, and over the bank I go,
Safe to circle the pond, cause the water is solidly froze,
Out of the spillway, and back into the field,
With the barb-wire fence in sight, it's time to yield,
Now, the fun over, it's time to trek back to the top,
So, the next sledder can run, and onto the sled quickly hop,
What else can I say,
But what a fun way to spend a snow day!

Ronnie "The Poet" Hammond
12-25-16

"Santa's Elves"

They're short and look pretty mean
but trust me, they're not fiends,
Rather, they are makers of toys and dreams
their pay is when a child's face beams
They work around the clock
and someone else's work they never mock,
Working all year long
they usually whistle a song,
Clothed in red and green
they're a sight to see,
Working with haste
not using glue or paste,
Wearing long pointed caps and bells on their toes
you can hear them coming wherever you go,
So when you open your present and get a toy,
don't forget to pay the elves by showing them joy!

Ronnie "The Poet" Hammond
12-13-96

"The Christmas Tree"

Tall, cylinder shaped, and dark green,
Lights wrap around it, while giving off a sparkle and beam,
Ornaments and decorations hang from the branches,
While presents sit below, is the big one mine, what are the chances?
A long, red ribbon also snakes its way around the tree,
While an angel sits on the very top, for all to see,
As pretty as a picture, in front of the window it stands,
For anyone to drive by, and admire as a Christmas lover and fan!

Ronnie "The Poet" Hammond
12-25-16

"A Spirit of Christmas"

Across the rooftops he sneaks
while children in bed, continue to sleep
Down the chimney he slips
with a gentle smile on his lips,
He strolls through the house to the tree
and presents, he leaves for free,
Then, he sits down by a stand to eat
the baked goods that are his treats,
After he eats, up the chimney he scoots
in his fancy red suit, and his, big, black boots
Finally, he climbs into his sleigh
thinking of how the children will play,
Although he's cold and the wind fiercely blows,
he continues on his trek,all names he carefully checks,
Until at last, all his presents are gone,
of a new day, its not even dawn,
Now its time to head back home to the pole
where on the fire, he adds some coal,
Then, he crawls into bed,
where he lays down his head,
And goes into a deep, sound sleep!

Ronnie "The Poet" Hammond
11-22-16

"Cowboy Frosty"

The kids begin to ball up, and roll the wet snow,
An overcast day, no wind yet blows,
The first snowball is made between knee, and waist tall,
It makes a strong base, to help prevent a fall,
Second comes a slightly smaller ball that sits on top of the first,
The kids remain warm, to finish will quench their thirst,
Continuing strong, a third and final ball is made,
Pushing, and heaving, once in place they let out a, "Hooray,
Sticks serve as arms, and a carrot for a nose,
Standing tall and proud, as the wind now blows,
Big, black buttons form the eyes,
Stones make up the smile, it's no lie,
Between the top two snowballs, a scarf is wrapped,
On top of the head is a cowboy hat, not a ball cap,
Finally, put on the stick arms, old, leather gloves are placed
Now, all that's needed is a name for the face,
"Cowboy Frosty," the kids all agree,
While their twinkling eyes, and bright smiles, make "Cowboy Frosty'
Seemingly smile with glee!

Ronnie "The Poet" Hammond
11-22-16

"The Reason for the Season?"

His parents traveling across country looking for a
place to stay,
turned away from everything except for a
manger with some hay.
Mary, pregnant, had rode on a donkey, and now
gave birth.
Three wise men camped on a hill followed a
bright star and gave them gifts, including myrrh.
The animals all watching, as if they knew,
a savior was born in the form of a babe so pure and new.
The child grew to be a carpenter and a fisher of men,
Who paid the ultimate price by dying for our sins.
So, while we celebrate with lights, gifts and decorated trees,
we need to give thanks, pray and really open
our eyes and get on our knees.
Remembering the true reason,
For this very special season!

Ronnie "The Poet" Hammond
12-05-21

"To All"

Years ago the Pilgrims rowed to the shore of
Plymouth Rock,
They settled and built homes and a dock.
The natives pitched in and helped
touching the Pilgrims hearts and how they felt,
So in turn they invited their friends to a feast and
celebration,
Thus,"Thanksgiving" was born, and is continued
today,
with friends, family and other relations.
A time to have fellowship, good food and to reflect
on loved ones already gone, ones to come
along and memories to recall or detect.
Therefore, no matter if the weather feels like,
spring or fall,
A safe and Happy Thanksgiving I wish to you all!

Ronnie "The Poet" Hammond
11-21-21

"A Tale of Thanks"

Across the sea from England
seeking land, a home and not fame,
They landed at Plymouth Rock
although there was no dock,
Their feet touched firm land
instead of warm, soft sand,
Quickly they began to build their homes
not knowing that they were not alone,
They had native friends nearby
that knew how to live and survive,
•So after illness, death, and bad luck
they came to help, through the forest mud and muck,
Then, they taught the newcomers to plant crops
and the year was not a flop,
Happy to be healthy and living
they invited their native friends over for a meal of Thanksgiving,
Now it is known as Thanksgiving Day
and what a great story, wouldn't you say!?

Ronnie "The Poet" Hammond
11-4-97

"Halloween Night"

On October 3 1st of each year
here's a night that in the hearts of children strikes fear,
It begins at dark
when coyotes start to howl and bark,
The moon rises full and bright
and to small children it's an eerie sight,
It's a time for ghosts to rise from their graves
and banshee's to rant and rave,
For witches to straddle their brooms and fly
into the evening sky,
And for creatures of the dark
to strike, and leave their mark,
As for children, they must be bold
and march from house to house in the cold,
Fore, at each house they knock, and yell "Trick or Treat"
there are goodies of all varieties to eat,
And after they forget their fright
they'll always remember "Halloween Night"

Ronnie "The Poet" Hammond
1994

IV.
Patriotic

"A Symbol of Freedom"

High in the sky waving proud and true,
covered with stars and stripes, red, white and blue.
A symbol of freedom to be shared by all,
throughout the battles of time, it never falls.
It has flown high in the jungle, the desert, and on the beach,
When sought by villains and conquerors, it remains out of reach.
The flag should remain tidy and fit,
cause our forefathers died protecting it.
So next time you pass a flag, whipping in the wind
think of your forefathers, stand proud, and call it friend!

Ronnie "The Poet" Hammond
09-28-95

"Freedom's Not Free"

Throughout history wars have been fought,
lives injured or lost, is the price for freedom bought.
From the Civil War, to World War One and Two, and even Desert Storm,
Someone always loses, no matter their size or alliances formed.
Fighting for a cause or a belief,
Thankful when the fighting ends, but not everyone is relieved,
Waiting for loved ones to come home alive,
sadly though, some come home injured, but many don't survive.
They do this for their country, and the red, white and blue,
"Memorial Day is to honor them and their memories, it's true!
Not just for barbecues, beer and fishin'
so I pray that to my words you'll listen.
'Fore some gave all, and all gave some for what they believe
but unfortunately,
"Freedom is Not Free!"

Ronnie "The Poet" Hammond
05-30-21

"The Flag"

High in the sky waving proud and true,

Covered with stars and stripes, red white, and blue,

A symbol of freedom to be shared by all,

Throughout the battles of time, it never falls,

It has flown high in the jungle, the desert, and on the beach,

When sought by villains and conquerors, it remains out of reach,

The flag should remain tidy and fit,

'Cause our forefathers died protecting it,

So next time you pass a flag whipping in the wind,

Think of your forefathers, stand proud, and call it friend!

Ronnie "The Poet" Hammond
9-28-95

"Memorial Day"

There is one day each year,
that we celebrate without any fear.
This freedom was fought and paid for by our armed forces,
by many means of transportation, be it planes, tanks, subs and even horses.
Some gave all and all gave some, when all was said and done,
Many came home injured and scared, others never came back, no, it was not fun.
Thankful to all of the sacrifices made by each one,
as they fought for our freedoms in the sands, prairies, mountains, and even the sky,
beneath the sun.
We all need to remember the real reason for this holiday, no it's not the day off or cookouts,
but to remember the sacrifices and military personnel that kept us free, and not living in fear is what it's about.
So, as you celebrate this very special holiday, be thankful and pray.
For everyone that fought and sacrificed so that we could celebrate, "Memorial Day"!

Ronnie "The Poet" Hammond
05-26-24

"Be Aware"

Some people today take too many things for granted,
even thinking things should be their way and even demanded.
Not flying flags, saluting, nor thanking our veterans for their sacrifices,
that allow us to live free, often times no thinking about the price
Loved ones lost, killed or maimed,
some with nothing left of their remains but a name.
Others come home but are never quite the same,
problems fitting in, shakes, night mares, but placing no blames.
From the Civil War where brother fought brother,
families divided with scared and grieving Mothers.
landing on the beaches of Normandy under heavy fire.
For a soldier to say he wasn't scared would make him a liar,
World War I and II left the whole world in worry and prayer.
Worried about the outcome left everyone scared,
as other wars and battles come and hopefully go,
the outcome only God truly knows.
So, we as Americans need to think about the costs of winning,
quit being selfish and stop sinning,
Give praise to the Lord and respect our veterans and the flag,
if you have family that are veterans feel free to brag!
Like Billy Ray Cyrus sang "All Gave Some, and Some Gave All"

"Be Aware"
(Continued)

Some were drafted while others answered the call!
Cold, hungry, wet, wounded, captured or alone
they fought for their freedoms, rights and to
protect this country and their home.
To all the veterans that have come and gone,
all I can say, is "Thank-You" and "God Bless the USA"!

Ronnie "The Poet" Hammond
05/08/2022

V.
Inspiring Words

"The Cross"

Standing against the sky

while people stopped walking by

The sun glaring,

they stood staring!

While the Lord hung in pain,

with nothing to gain,

He paid our way

with little to say

Until at last when we were freed,

by HIS dying need!

Ronnie "The Poet" Hammond
SBU, 1993
First religious poem ever written by me.

"How Will It Sound"

Whether you're with family, friends, or all alone,
or you've been "called" home and are
standing before the throne.
When God speaks to you, how will it be,
will it sound like waves crashing on the sea?
Or soothing, like water trickling in a stream,
could it sound like a voice from a dream?
Like thunder, will it boom,
shaking your house and every room?
Perhaps it will sound like a whisper in the wind
and both of your ears you'll want to lend.
Might it echo from the mountains and across the plains,
or be refreshing like a misting rain?
Maybe in different volumes and tones it will resound,
think about it, "How will it sound?"

Ronnie "The Poet" Hammond
03/19/2022

"Riding for God's Brand"

Up every day with the rising of the sun,
To take care of business, and maybe have some fun,
Shaved, showered, and dressed in his western attire,
A man of his word, it's out the door to do the chores,
On the farm there's always something to do, with seldom a bore,
After choring he saddles his horse to check cattle and fence,
Praying for forgiveness for his sins, and willing to repent,
A leather cross hangs from his saddle as he rides along,
Whistling a tune, and a song,
Tending to business from dawn to dusk,
He has God, no need for luck,
For God's glory, he'll always make a stand,
Because like an old west cattle drover, he's riding for Gods Brand.

Ronnie "The Poet" Hammond
12-13-2020

"A Wrangler of Men"

Soft spoken and a cowboy to loot,
Wearing jeans, shirts, hat, and boots,
Laid back and normally with a positive outlook,
Every day he reads verses from, "the good book",
Whenever the opportunity arises,
No matter who it is, or where at, it'll not be a surprise,
To spread God's word, and to teach about salvation,
He'll spend any amount of time needed, with no reservation,
Like an old time hired hand on a ranch,
God is in his life and heart by choice, and not chance,
Telling them how they can be forgiven of their sins,
This Godly man is a true wrangler of men!

Ronnie "The Poet" Hammond
12-13-2020

"Take the Reins"

If the world is weighing on your shoulders,
Trying to weigh you down like a ton of boulders.
You've tied a knot in the end of your rope,
Hanging on for dear life, about to lose all hope,
The sky is dark and full of gloom,
And you feel like your facing, "Dr. Doom."
You think there's no hope in sight,
But all you have to do is look for the light.
Your cries and prayers will not be in vain,
If, like a true cowboy, you let God "Take the Reins'!

Ronnie "The Poet" Hammond
(06-06-21)

"Be Joyful"

God has a plan for us, I believe,
Try to be receptive to His plan, and you will receive.
Have your prayers been heard, you may wonder,
because for an answer you hunger.
To remain positive and open-minded can be hard to do,
sometimes your uplifted, mad or even blue.
Things may become difficult, or even go awry,
leaving you stressed, worried, or ready to cry.
However, if you truly believe and your faith is not fake,
There is no trial or tribulation that can cause it to break.
So, allow your faith to be strong,
knowing that God still loves us even if we do wrong.
Lift your voice up in song and prayer,
Tell the "unknowing" that His love is safe, they
need not beware
Don't be afraid to talk to strangers or take a chance,
Share a laugh, smile or even a dance.
Remaining loyal, steadfast and thoughtful,
the fact that God has a plan for us, should
remind us to "Be Joyful"!

Ronnie "The Poet" Hammond
06-20-21

"United and True"

Being a Christian isn't easy at times,
Satan has bad stuff on TV, radio, T-Shirts and signs.
Causing us to sometimes backslide a step or two,
letting our guard slip some can be easy to do.
Standing alone, we may stumble, or even fall,
however, if we stand together, Satan can
never defeat us all.
So, try and find someone to help hold you
accountable in your life,
Whether it be a friend, husband, co-worker, or wife
This way Satan can't trick us into taking a fall,
If we stand True, United and Tall!

Ronnie "The Poet" Hammond
09-04-21

"A New Dawning"

Every morning the sun rises in the east like a fire ablaze,
always steadily rising and bright, unlike the moon in a phase.
Bring forth light to the world along with warmth and heat,
helping plants to grow, allowing wildlife food to eat.
Allowing people to feel better and happy in its' rays,
whether on the plains, or a mountain or by a bay.
Just an easy reminder of God's handiwork and steadfast love,
Pretty as a blooming flower or a snow-white dove.
An obvious testament to the phase, "a dawning of
a new day"
so make time to watch a sunrise and you'll be amazed!
It will open you eyes in awe, and there will be no yawning,
if you watch and see "A New Dawning"

Ronnie "The Poet" Hammond
11-21-21

"Answer His Call"

It may come to you in a vision or dream,
a sign that no one but you can see that in your
eyes leaves a gleam.
A voice so soft and kind that whispers in your ear,
leaving you overjoyed, but without any fear.
An undetectable hand, that touches your shoulder,
strengthening you to the point that you feel as
if you could lift a boulder.
Someone reaching out to you through a phone call
or a stranger stopping to help you out when
you feel like you're about to fall.
So regardless of where you're at, be it lost in a
maze, or wandering down a never-ending hall.
Have faith, be assured, and "Answer His Call"!

Ronnie "The Poet" Hammond
03-05-23

"It's True"

Sometimes the weather is so hot and dry
that you feel like your skins about to fry.
Or it can be freezing cold with snow,
while the wind so fiercely blows.
People think that Mother Nature controls it all,
but I believe that it's due to another's call.
Remember that God created everything that we
can see, touch or taste,
and He did so with little or no waste,
Yes, I believe in Mother Nature too,
however, God is the almighty one, "It's True"!

Ronnie “The Poet” Hammond
01-09-22

"Precious Gifts From God"

They may not have things that we take for granted
the ability to talk, only to yell or almost chant.
To be able to walk, skip, hop or jump,
or give a friend a celebratory chest or fist bump.
Eager to learn and make family proud,
and in a natural way, stand out in a crowd.
To drive, date and be a productive member of society,
while many never will, don't be sad and cry
Even like the ones in Garth Brooks video for
"Standing Outside the Fire"
God loves them each and everyone, He is not a liar!
They are precious gifts from God and can help with many tasks,
From bringing families closer together, to
sharing how love can be kept alive and forever last.
So, please do not be embarrassed or ashamed,
do not accuse your spouse or onto God put the blame.
Love and enjoy them as much as you can,
because you'll see them again in Heaven, as
beside Him they'll stand!

Ronnie Hammond
04/23/2022

"An Awesome God"

Have you ever watched the sunrise at dawn,
or saw a doe tending to her newborn fawn.
Sat in awe a the size and beauty of the mountains,
listened to the falling water spilling out of a fountain.
Felt the under toll of the ocean as it pulled on your feet,
denied the Devil's suggestions, sending him away in defeat.
Played in the freshly fallen snow,
or in a hay field felt a warm breeze blow.
Danced in the softly falling rain,
or by praying to God, found relief from pain.
Walked down a sidewalk and from a stranger,
received a smile and a nod,
if you have done any or all of these,
then you already know that we have an awesome God!

Ronnie Hammond
05/27/2022

"Thankful"

Negativity is all around us in the world today
from horn honking, to hand gestures, and
things people say.
All of these things tend to bring us down,
and instead of wearing a smile, it turns into a frown.
To some things we even turn a blind eye,
by cheating, stealing, or telling a lie.
We must remember that we wear the armor of the Lord,
and thus, there is no need for anger, taking up
arms or even a sword.
A plan for us one and all, he already has in play,
His word however is final and not just hearsay.
So, we must hold ourselves accountable as we follow our path,
while standing tall spreading His word and not tempting His wrath,
Providing things, we need from day to day,
and giving us the words to use and say.
We should be thankful for His undying love,
while we strive to remain as pure as a snow-white dove.

Ronnie "The Poet" Hammond
05-23-21

"He Loves Cowboys"

While thinking about cowboys the other day,
Their attire and its uses came into play,
Who came up with these ideas and there uses,
Helping cowboys stay safe while not blowing fuses,
The answer is God the creator,
He is a lover, not a hater
Cowboy hats provide shade and even from the heat,
Bandanna's protect from air borne things and look neat,
Long sleeve shirts save arms from sunburns and even brush,
While chasing cattle in a hurried rush,
The same can be said for blue jeans,
No matter if they're dirty or clean,
Boots of fine leather protect toes, feet and shins,
Feeling good while wearing them, cowboys can't help but grin,
It doesn't matter if your name is not Gene, John, or Roy
Because you see, He loves all cowboys!

Ronnie "The Poet" Hammond
5/1/21

"Called To"

Pastors come from all walks of life,
widowed, single or with a wife.
Coming from homes that were happy, broken, or none at all,
some successful in business, some however,
having been hit and taken a fall.
Laborers, farmers, and ever wrestlers it's true,
have risen from hardships, addictions, and feeling blue,
Find salvation and giving themselves to the Lord,
being re-born, now a child of God, safer and
stronger this any concrete ever poured
Race, color, handicaps or disabilities are never a
hindrance it's true,
for those special people that are "Called To!"

Ronnie "The Poet" Hammond
03-12-23

"How Will It Be?"

When our time on Earth is through,
with our passing, loved ones and friends will
be sad and blue.
However upwards to Heaven we will ascend,
a new journey we will begin!
With bodies anew, and no suffering or pain!
Oh, the glories we will have and gain!
Will the streets be made of gold?
perfect weather, no hot or freezing cold?
Soft, fluffy, strong wings will we use to fly;
able to sit with God, by HIS side?
Beautiful flowing garments will we wear,
no more temptation, sin or crosses to bear!
Perfect halos floating above our heads.
made of an unknown substance, but definitely not lead!
Loved ones that have gone before us might we see,
I truly do wonder, just "How Will It Be?"

Ronnie "The Poet" Hammond
04-09-23

"Miracles Never Cease"

In times of stress and despair,
your strength and courage, He will replenish and repair.
Odds may appear over whelming and unbeatable,
having faith and believing, he will keep you undefeatable.
Storms may rage and oceans roll,
He is with us always and will guide us safely across the atoll.
Night fall may seem to be never ending,
a good night's rest He can grant us, there is no "pending"!
Anything that we may have to face, and think that there's no escape or release,
Just remember that His "Miracles Never Cease"!

Ronnie "The Poet" Hammond
04-23-23

"Let Him Drive"

As we travel down our daily roads,
there is trash, pot holes and heavy loads.
Causing us to be nervous, scared and have doubts,
getting mad, yelling or on the verge of a pout,
Slowing down, swerving, taking the ditch, or even
stopping.
Firmly grasping the wheel with both hands about
to blow your top,
What shall be done about all of this from day to day?
We can continue and make a wish or we can pray!
Just because we cannot physically touch HIM
doesn't mean that He's not alive,
And with him beside us, we will be safe and
sound if only we "Let Him Drive"!

Ronnie "The Poet" Hammond
03-19-23

"My Blessed Gift"

From a young age, in English class in school,
I was drawn to poems that rhymed and sounded cool!
Pursuing them I began to write my own,
never once giving up, or wanting to fold.
Sharing my poems in times of good and bad,
whether or not, I was happy or sad.
Something always just pops in my head and the
words begin to flow,
like a stream, their coming is steady but slow
Other times they rush out, like a busted damn
leaving me thinking, man it felt like someone
was guiding my hand
I have no doubt that God has blessed me with this
talent and gift.
So that through my poems, people's spirit I may lift.
To provide a different perspective or way of thinking,
Bringing people to His word, with a poetic link.
So, with the words that God gives me, I try to fill a rift,
while praising Him and touching people with
"My Blessed Gift!

Ronnie "The Poet" Hammond
03-05-23

"Stand Tall and True"

No matter where you go, evil can be found,
liars, cheaters and such people abound
Suggestive scenes on TV, unnecessary words in lyrics of a song,
things being cooked and made, that in our lives don't belong.
Stampedes at concerts, also shootings in schools,
road rage, street fighting, and people just
acting the part of a fool.
We, that know and love the Lord, have nothing to fear,
nor do those that we hold dear.
For HE provides us with armor and everything else
that we need,
reminding us to live by our faith and His love,
allowing other people to see.
Just how great and mighty HE truly is,
and how too they can bathe in His love and not just wish.
No matter if you're well or sick, happy, or sad and blue,
All we have to do is believe and
"Stand Tall and True"!

Ronnie "The Poet" Hammond
04-16-23

"Throughout The Years"

Throughout the years, Gods word has lasted in
different versions and prints,
It is the truth and the way, and has brought
people to repent,
All over the world it can be found
pages stand proudly bound.
During times of famine, diseases and wars,
whether you're of nobility, or just a person who's poor.
As long as you have the Holy Bible and believe its words
Being freed from any string, chains or cords.
A true believer that has been saved, can live all
365 days without fear,
Just as the Bible has survived, and will continue to do so
"Throughout the Years!"

Ronnie "The Poet" Hammond
03-12-23

"To Ascend"

Heaven is where we all want to go,
floating on clouds, not burning forever down below.
However, our ticket cannot be purchased by deeds,
money or tokens,
but, once purchased it can never be taken
away or broken.
Our lives, hearts and souls given to God obediently
fending off the devil and his temptations relentlessly,
Armed with the armor of God and His never-ending love,
Someday we will fly to Heaven as pure as a
snow-white dove!
Changing our ways, while walking our path,
regardless of its twists or bends,
as a child of God, we will be prepared
"To Ascend"!

Ronnie "The Poet" Hammond
03-26-23

"What Will You Say?"

When your race is finally run,

with no more pain, weariness, joy or fun.,

Your time on Earth is over and through,

to answer for you sins, before you're born anew

At the pearly gates you will stand with Saint Peter

while he checks for your name,

If you know the Lord and given your life to

HIM, Peter will smile and say, "you finally came!"

Nobody knows when this time will be,

Or how great and wonderful it will feel being

completely free.

So, whether its next week, next month, next year

or even today,

Are you ready, and do you know

"What Will You Say?"

Ronnie "The Poet" Hammond
04-02-23

"Turn the Page"

Do you ever feel exhausted or totally alone?
wishing for energy, or maybe even a clone?
At the end of you rope, desperately clinging on to
the knot, feeling as useless as an ink dot?
Overwhelmed with no end in sight,
dark as a tunnel with no light?
How can you ever overcome all of these things?
there's no need for any tablet, computer, or
phone that rings.
Do not let Satan or anything have power over you,
where you feel trapped in a cage,
just pick up the BIBLE, read, and
<u>"Turn the Page!"</u>

Ronnie "The Poet" Hammond
04-23-23

"One of God's Tools"

He gave you parents that raised you to be strong,
honest, hardworking, and with the knowledge
of right and wrong.
Over the years, you have continued to prosper
and grow, through good times and bad, also
times of highs and lows.
Never giving up, or losing your beliefs and faith,
knowing that God has a plan, and that He is
the ultimate foundation or base.
Continuing to grow and teach His word,
Like a shepherd with his flock, not like a
drover and a herd.
Willing to lead people to Him, no matter where
they are,
whether they are local, or come from afar.
Helping families grow closer, or performing a
baptism in the water,
He'll stand tall and true, not one to falter.
Along with this poem comes appreciation and
something I have to say,
I hope you have a very blessed, and Happy Birthday!
A good ole boy, that's definitely not a fool,
There's no doubt however that He's
"One of God's tools"!

Ronnie "The Poet" Hammond
04-23-22

"Breaker of Chains"

Sometimes it feels like your feet are shackled and bound,
feeling like you cannot escape your pursuers
and the hounds.
Your hands feel heavy, like they're cuffed and not
able to use,
leaving your spirit and will power weak and confused.
An invisible yoke seems to surround you head and shoulders,
weighing heavily upon you like a huge boulder
You try to continue on, not knowing what else to do,
weaker and weaker, slipping into despair and
feeling blue.
Until at last you collapse and end up on your knees,
but then you are lifted up and the shackles
and chains are removed by a force unseen.
God has seen you plight and reached down to set you free.
All you need to do is pray and believe,
because just like He made the sun, moon,
snow and rain,
Also, is He a "Breaker of Chains"!

Ronnie "The Poet" Hammond
04/03/2022

"Give It All Away"

Some people seem to handle anything that comes their way,
seemingly upbeat and positive with nothing
negative to say.
Others however try to shoulder life's burdens,
while trying to stand not wanting to give in
and on their knees land.
People often wonder what to do,
to try and weather their storm and not be blue.
The devil's temptations are only a temporary fix,
and with a person's heart and soul are not a good mix.
A person can struggle on or put on a fake show,
talk to family and friends and continue to go
with the flow
The best thing is to tell the Lord everything with
the words you say, and to Him, just give it all away!

Ronnie “The Poet” Hammond
06/12/2022

"The True Captain"

Like sailors in times of old,
braving the seas and oceans no matter the
heat, storms, or cold.
No modern equipment or comforts to help them along,
with a feeling inside, them telling them that they belong.
With only a compass and stars to help them navigate,
just their shipmates with whom to congregate.
Hard labor or toils during the day,
sore and exhausted at night, probably with no one to pray.
Sickness and storms along with shortages of food and water,
These that reach their destination gave thanks to the Father.
The creator of everything and everyone, He always has a plan,
He can calm any storms with a word or a
motion causing the water to be calm as land
So, you never need to have worry or fear,
lose your faith or break down in tears.
God's Will shall be done, so no matter what may happen,
have faith and never fear, for God is the True Captain!

Ronnie "The Poet" Hammond
04/10/2022

"Just Walk Away"

The devil tries to trap us each and every day,
thoughts we think, things we see and words people say.
We try to remain strong and true,
but sometimes it's not so easy to do.
The devil never stops, he's always on the move,
constantly trying to slow our role, or interrupt our groove
He hammers on us the hardest when we're all alone,
from things on the radio, TV and on cell phones.
Knowing no one is with us to watch our backs,
hoping we'll give in because support is what we lack,
However, the Lord is with us day and night, 24/7
and has a place for us waiting in Heaven!
So when we are tempted by the devils sway,
We simply hold our heads up high, and
"Just Walk Away"!

Ronnie "The Poet" Hammond
04-18-21

"Like A Farmer"

Just like a farmer works up the ground,
and scatters seeds among the dirt clods and mounds.
Praying for rain to start a growth,
with a tap root and greening up both.
Sunshine along with some "TLC"
you'll be surprised when it grows, at what you see.
The Lord does the same for us,
remember, man was made from dirt and dust,
Giving us a solid foundation, along with
everything we need,
His word and laws we should always heed.
After His work is done., He waits to reap what He SOWS
Have faith and read the Bible and it will tell you all
you need to know.
So, follow His example and stay on the right path
while His children will grow like numbers in math.
Strong roots that run deep, is what we need,
and living a Christian lifestyle will keep out the weeds.
Numbered from birth, your days may be,
and after our last day, the Lord we'll get to see!

Ronnie "The Poet" Hammond
02/27/22

"Prove Me Wrong"

When life throws you a curve or unexpected things happen,
your mood is low, and your spirits appear to dampen,
The sky seems to be dark and dreary,
worn out you feel weary.
Help and guidance are what you need,
God's word can be used for your soul to feed.
Prayer and the Bible can help guide you along,
remember, God loves us all, just try and prove me wrong!

Ronnie "The Poet" Hammond
03/05/2022

"Take the Wheel"

Sometimes the world seems to be spinning at an unreal pace,
trials and difficulties arise that we must face.
Whether sitting at home or walking down the street,
we get weary and begin to think about defeat.
Our will power, belief and strength begin to fade,
often, we choose to follow the devils' ways.
Smoking, drugging or with alcohol trying to drown our sorrows,
sinking deeper into despair with our troubles
no wanting to ask for help or anything to borrow.
Until at last, no more do we think we can take,
finally, we ask God for help before it's too late.
On bended knees with hands folded tight
we pray that if it's His will, He'll lead us back into the light.
Like doctors' work to keep us healthy,
and investors try to make us wealthy.
Or a chef prepares for us an extravagant meal,
like a designated driver, the Lord will handle
our problems and take us home safely if we
ask Him to take the wheel!

Ronnie "The Poet" Hammond
03/12/2022

"In Our Fathers Home"

On Sunday morning we go to the "Living Waters Church"
listening intently like a bird on a perch.
The fellowship team and band bring songs of praise,
while voices and spirits begin to raise.
A strong, solid message follows it up,
overflowing from God's always knowledgeable Cup.
Eyes closed, heads bowed, and prayers made
said with conviction and love, never to fade.
It makes no difference of our past sins or if were alone,
as long as we come with open eyes and hearts
into our Fathers Home!

Ronnie “The Poet” Hammond
04/02/2022

"Our Loving Father"

Sometimes you get caught up in everyday life,
with work, kids, a husband or a wife.
Evenings and weekends are spent trying to get
things caught up and done,
stress and tension mount, with no time for fun.
Feeling burnt out and at the end of your rope,
your energy level dwindles, as does your faith and hope.
Luckily, the Lord loves us and knows what we need,
to Him we just need to listen, and His words we heed.
He gave us land, water, trees and sky
allowing us to hike, boat and climb, it's no lie!
Communing with nature, recharging our batteries
and taking a break
Renews our spirit while keeping us real and not
someone fake.
So, you see it's really no bother,
Because the Lord is our Loving Father

Ronnie “The Poet” Hammond
04/02/2022

"Return To The River"

As the world continues to fall and spiral into the dark,
people doing bad things during the day, night,
in buildings and parks.
Murder drugs, theft and abuse,
however, Gods children won't give in, they refuse.
Continuing to believe and support His word,
no matter the teasing, laughing or goating.
He is the almighty Giver!
We just need to continue to pray and return to the river!
To let the water cleanse us again,
all we need to do to begin,
since He is the almighty Giver,
we just need to continue to pray and return to the river!

Ronnie "The Poet" Hammond
04/10/2022

"Surprise Blessings"

Often times things happen that catch is by surprise
maybe even scaring us, it's no lie.
Examples range from an unexpected call, to
finding money on the ground
finding a really good buy, to seeing a buck on the bound.
A friend from years gone by, reaching out to you,
storms blowing over leaving behind a sky of blue
Sadness turning to happiness from the lyric of a song,
or the tranquility of a calm and quiet pond
Some may say these things cannot be explained
you understand why,
to convince them is useless no matter how hard you try.
But I know the real reason, there's no need for guessing,
It's just one of God's many Surprise Blessings!

Ronnie "The Poet" Hammond
05/08/2022

"Like a Potter"

God created is in His image, and until our death He
is not done,
He is always with us, while we are crying or having fun.
Like a potter with clay, water and a spinning wheel,
God created us, and gave us receptors, so we can feel.
Buds for us to taste with, and legs to stand upon or flee.
Arms to carry loads, and eyes that allow us to see.
A nose to smell and breathe, and ears to hear,
our brain to hold knowledge, and a sense of fear.
Mouths allow us to eat and talk,
While our feet help us to walk.
Voices to let us talk, sing and praise God,
And we all have our own style of bod.
So many other wonders He has blessed us with,
From height, to smarts, or the ability to safely dive from a cliff.
In His image we are all made,
even in later age when these things change and begin to fade.
A plan for us all He has, for He is our almighty Father,
and patient and talented "Like a Potter"!

Ronnie "The Poet" Hammond
11-28-21

Made in the USA
Columbia, SC
08 September 2024

41447442R00059